Hotel Restaurant Bar Club Design

Architecture + Interiors Designed by Studio GAIA

Hotel Restaurant Bar Club Design

Architecture + Interiors Designed by Studio GAIA

Foreword by **Jonathan Morr** Introduction and Text by **Andrew Yang**

Visual Reference Publications Inc.

Visual Reference Publications, Inc.
302 Fifth Avenue
New York, NY 10001

Distributors to the trade in the United States and Canada:
Watson-Guptill
770 Broadway
New York, NY 10003

Distributors outside the United States and Canada:
HarperCollins International
10 East 53rd Street
New York, NY 10022-5299

This book is exclusively distributed in China
By Beijing Designerbooks Co., Ltd.
Building No. 2, No. 3 Babukou Gulouxidajie
Xicheng District, Beijing 100009, P.R. China
Tel: 0086(010)6406-7653
Fax: 0086(010)6406-0931
E-mail: info@designerbooks.net
http://www.designerbooks.net

Library of Congress Cataloging in Publication Data:
Hotel • Bar • Restaurant • Club Design

ISBN 1-58471-100-0

Printed in China

Contents

To my wife Ronit and my kids, Gaia, Leeor and Noam, for their support of my passion.

Ilan Waisbrod

Foreword

When Ilan asked me to write the introduction to his first book, I was honored... and terrified. I'm not a writer. I'm not an architecture critic. I'm a restauranteur, a client, a collaborator, and a friend. I gave his request some thought. Yes, it actually makes sense: Ilan and I started our independent careers together. My first solo restaurant was his first solo design project. I'm honored that he chose me to introduce you to his work.

Before I opened my own restaurant, Ilan and I had been friends for years, and I had always appreciated his architectural integrity and instinctive feeling for strong, emotional design. I was certain that as soon as I was able to do a project on my own, Ilan would be the architect.

My first opportunity came with Republic, a high-energy noodle emporium on Union Square in New York City. Ilan's design was an instant success. He took a challenging space and transformed it into one of the most talked-about restaurants in New York. The furniture, lighting and architecture – all Ilan's responsibility - combined to create an environment of tremendous impact. Republic took the city and the restaurant industry by storm – restauranteurs flew in from around the country to check out the new sensation.

Our next project was Bond Street, a chic multi-level sushi restaurant in New York's emerging NoHo neighborhood. The space has sense of ethereality, restraint and romance perfectly suited to the restaurant's concept and clientele. In this case, Ilan went more for feeling than architectural fireworks. At first glance, the visual link between Republic and Bond Street might not be apparent, but it is a mark of Ilan's creativity and sensibility that he approaches each project on its own terms, without the constraint of specific architectural language.

These two restaurants - the projects that, for both of us, represented intensely personal first steps on the road to success - were not only innovative and exciting at the time, but today, nearly a decade later, are equally fresh. Ilan's designs became instant classics, and both places have easily stood the test of time in the ever-fickle world of New York restaurants.

Ilan has since evolved into a major international architect. His projects include hotels, restaurants, and private homes. You can find his work around the globe, from New York to Mexico City to Seoul. As you'll see in this volume, the designer I spent nights working with to retool a two-thousand square-foot bar has blossomed into an architect with a distinctive, subtly discernable personal style, responsible for projects of tremendous scope. Studio Gaia, Ilan's company, is emerging as one of the pre-eminent architecture firms of our time. I am so proud of his journey.

Today, Ilan and I are collaborating on a new project. We feel like little kids again, staying at his office deep into the night, working yet again on a design that's small in scope but deeply meaningful to both of us. I constantly marvel and his inventiveness and willingness to embrace new ideas. I look forward to continuing our wonderful collaboration – and friendship – for many years to come.

Jonathan Morr

Vaishali Patel   Kanako Fukuda   Garrett Robbins   Susana Simonpietri   Patricia Walker   Peggy Leung

Ilan Waisbrod   Saira Jacob   Ronald Deschamp   Heaohn Lee   Elise Lee

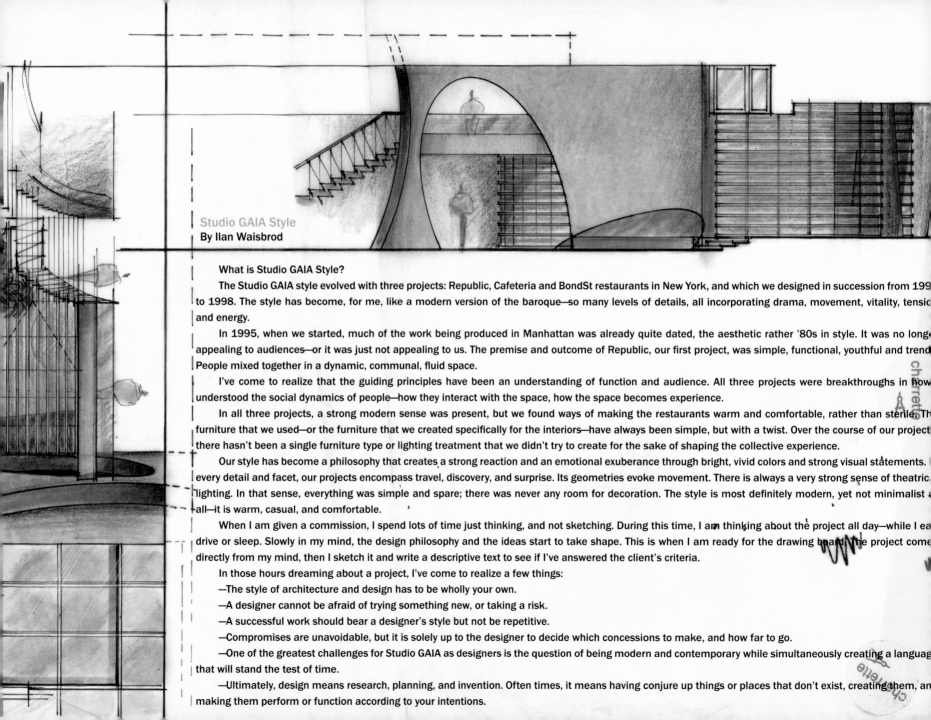

Studio GAIA Style
By Ilan Waisbrod

What is Studio GAIA Style?

The Studio GAIA style evolved with three projects: Republic, Cafeteria and BondSt restaurants in New York, and which we designed in succession from 199_ to 1998. The style has become, for me, like a modern version of the baroque—so many levels of details, all incorporating drama, movement, vitality, tensio_ and energy.

In 1995, when we started, much of the work being produced in Manhattan was already quite dated, the aesthetic rather '80s in style. It was no long_ appealing to audiences—or it was just not appealing to us. The premise and outcome of Republic, our first project, was simple, functional, youthful and trend_ People mixed together in a dynamic, communal, fluid space.

I've come to realize that the guiding principles have been an understanding of function and audience. All three projects were breakthroughs in how_ understood the social dynamics of people—how they interact with the space, how the space becomes experience.

In all three projects, a strong modern sense was present, but we found ways of making the restaurants warm and comfortable, rather than sterile. Th_ furniture that we used—or the furniture that we created specifically for the interiors—have always been simple, but with a twist. Over the course of our project_ there hasn't been a single furniture type or lighting treatment that we didn't try to create for the sake of shaping the collective experience.

Our style has become a philosophy that creates a strong reaction and an emotional exuberance through bright, vivid colors and strong visual statements. _ every detail and facet, our projects encompass travel, discovery, and surprise. Its geometries evoke movement. There is always a very strong sense of theatric_ lighting. In that sense, everything was simple and spare; there was never any room for decoration. The style is most definitely modern, yet not minimalist a_ all—it is warm, casual, and comfortable.

When I am given a commission, I spend lots of time just thinking, and not sketching. During this time, I am thinking about the project all day—while I ea_ drive or sleep. Slowly in my mind, the design philosophy and the ideas start to take shape. This is when I am ready for the drawing board. The project come_ directly from my mind, then I sketch it and write a descriptive text to see if I've answered the client's criteria.

In those hours dreaming about a project, I've come to realize a few things:

—The style of architecture and design has to be wholly your own.

—A designer cannot be afraid of trying something new, or taking a risk.

—A successful work should bear a designer's style but not be repetitive.

—Compromises are unavoidable, but it is solely up to the designer to decide which concessions to make, and how far to go.

—One of the greatest challenges for Studio GAIA as designers is the question of being modern and contemporary while simultaneously creating a languag_ that will stand the test of time.

—Ultimately, design means research, planning, and invention. Often times, it means having conjure up things or places that don't exist, creating them, an_ making them perform or function according to your intentions.

In the beginning of the 21st Century, Studio GAIA had an opportunity to design, from top to bottom, two major hotels in South Korea and Mexico. In the projects for W Mexico City and W Seoul, the details and beliefs of Studio GAIA really came together. Everything, with regard to furniture, details, materials, and audience, was a culmination of everything that we had done so far. Both projects were visual, but dressed up; refined, but simple; chic, but not overdone. The design made its own statement and did not mimic other styles.

For W Mexico City, we traveled to Mexico to learn the culture, habits, history, materials fashion, and colors that are native to the country. When were there, we stayed near the Parque de Chapultepec, at the Camino Real. One of the classic masterpieces by Mexican modernist Ricardo Legorreta, the Camino Real has stood the test of time and became a real touchstone for what we hoped to do with W Mexico City.

And what did we learn about making a luxury hotel? We've learned that hotels must be a place where the traveler can obtain privacy and relaxation at his or her destination. A home away from home, certainly, but a night in this hotel should be like an overnight stay in an art museum—where, perhaps, the guest is treated like the artwork. Using colors, materials and shapes in ways that go beyond the ordinary, the hotel should be an innovative, dream-inspiring space.

We are living in an era where consumers' appetite for originality are increasing. People are after places that are intimate, comfortable, open, and ultimately, places that encourage togetherness. The first impressions of our hotels are always the entrances—part night club, part lobby. Immediately, one senses people all around. While this new model has elements of a club, the emphasis in our hotel design has always been on the quality of personal spaces such as bedrooms and bathrooms—which we've spent considerable energies on designing. All of which, in its disparate functions, should create a fantasy for the senses.

This is just one of the many ways of how design has dramatically changed the

hospitality industry today. It is one of the main reasons—if not the only reason—by which people choose a place to stay, or how they distinguish one brand from another. We travel to escape the daily routines of our lives and experience new sensations. With more leisure time and money available to spend on travel, easier options for reaching destinations, and a global business culture that is dependent on the world coming together, the travel industry has heated up in recent years, a very reflection of how dramatically life is different than they were 10 years ago.

The social diversification of recent years has generated new clients who are anxious for new projects and new ideas. Such a moment has created the desire for new establishments that offer personal attention, in not only service but also in material and spiritual comfort. The settings and ambiences enjoyed in these hotels are true celebrations of the senses, which stay with the traveler long after he or she has departed.

We've spent the last 10 years working hard to refine our brand, the Studio GAIA Style, and we hope that it's something that will remain with you as well.

Future Perfect: The Aesthetic of Studio GAIA
By Andrew Yang

My first encounter with a Studio GAIA interior—or at least what I thought was my first—happened at the W Seoul-Walkerhill. Arriving after spending more than 20 hours on a flight from New York, the connecting Airbus A330 plane from Tokyo landed late at night in Seoul's vast and futuristic airport. From the western coast of South Korea, the car zipped from the edge of South Korea and through the city, wending its way through on the north bank of the Han River, past the nearly 22 bridges before arriving at the eastern end of the city, where a

London, Paris or Rome—and in that moment no other place existed.

Since returning to New York, I promptly sought out those responsible for such a dynamic experience, which landed me at the door of Studio GAIA. The office, which numbered no more than a dozen people, has created some of the most beloved interiors throughout New York City. Beginning with Republic in 1996, which the office created for Jonathan Morr, then continuing on to such classics as Cafeteria in 1997, and BondSt in 1998, the Studio GAIA style, as practiced by founder and principal Ilan Waisbrod, had begun to coalesce into a style that was being cultivated into its own brand.

In a series of projects from 1996 through the ones currently in development in his studio, the aesthetic of Studio GAIA continues to become more pronounced, and bolder. For naïve observers, there are a few superficial characteristics one may observe about the office's work. First and foremost, there is the flair for bright colors–orange, apple red, lime green—bright colors, like those attributed Karim Rashid, although with none of the overstatement and ribald expressions of the industrial designer. There is the penchant for rounded corners, mod, space-like furnishings. Also, Studio GAIA projects are always incredibly stark, well-lit and photogenic. However, to reduce the

interiors to merely physical attributes would not quite do justice to the work.

The interiors of Studio GAIA are resolutely about the experience, about an urban statement that casts beliefs that are resoundingly Modern, in the Miesian sense of the word. This brand of design returns a refined Bauhaus approach to interiors. Just as a Barcelona pavilion came with its Barcelona chair, or a Brno house came with its Brno Chair, there is not a single aspect of a space—a new chair, a new lighting treatment, new seating banquettes—that Studio GAIA has not tried to readdress in one way or another, in order to shape the collective experience. Its ability to understand what clients—and what their audience—wants has led them to create, and then deliver, successful social spaces. A big part of that talent is an intimate understanding of how social animals like to congregate, and, in the case of Studio GAIA, an innate understanding of what's now, what's hip and what's chic.

Even in New York, where the expectations of experience are quite high from restaurants to hotels, firms have simply selected and picked sensible furnishings out of the Bernhardt and Knoll catalogs—some nice Saarinen chairs here, some Jacobsen stools there—Waisbrod continues to practice a bespoke brand of interior architecture. From small, 800-square-foot retail shops, to large, 15,000-square-feet club spaces, to 253-room hotels, Waisbrod has continued to be a provocateur in a highly competitive environment that has garnered it high-profile clients, and successful, long-standing projects.

However, as profilic as Studio GAIA has been since going into business in the past 10 years, the style continues to change and evolve. Where does it all come from? And what is driving it? The preternatural ability of the firm to create and shape some of the forms is confounding. Waisbrod has confessed a deep admiration for the architecture forms of Oscar Niemeyer, whose brand of modernism was more fluid and organic than those of his mid-century counterparts. And while

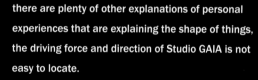

there are plenty of other explanations of personal experiences that are explaining the shape of things, the driving force and direction of Studio GAIA is not easy to locate.

"Sometimes when we're in the office, he'll say 'Look! Look! Look at what I did!'" says Peggy Leung, one of Studio GAIA's senior project architects. "And we'll rush over to see a drawing." There's a genuine, innate excitement about the potential of design, and the possibilities that it might generate, she says. That feeling of excitement continues to drive the firm. Of the principal's driving aesthetic, explains Leung, "It's that pureness of... I don't know what."

Born in 1961 in Israel, Ilan Waisbrod studied industrial and interior design at the Holon Institute of Technology at Tel Aviv University. At Tel Aviv, where he studied with Isaac Lepowitzky, a teacher that took part in the 1980s Memphis Group, a movement that included Ettore Sottsass

projects, it is, to this day, one of Studio GAIA's most influential projects, and nothing short of a revelation.

As an early work, Republic showed the penchant for color and an emphasis on creating both a functional, fluid space. The space was simple: a long, slight curving bar in front, with a large dining area in the back, with a kitchen tucked in between the two areas. As a business, the food and service was the fuel that powered the giant machine, architecture devised courtesy of Studio GAIA. The space has been absolutely critical to drive the business, and has been organized so that the dining area maximized the number of people that were able to be seated at once; the bar area, with its tall drink tables, sans chairs, created a comfortable environment for throngs of people waiting to eat. The downstairs space, another 2,800 square feet contained the offices, kitchen prep, and take-out operations. While other clients may take issue with the lack of a flexible space in the communal tables, the dining arrangement was just a part of the restaurant's package, part and parcel. It was really the best solution in creating a high-volume space.

Since creating Republic, the scales of Studio GAIA projects have become more complex, and the details more immense to manage. From the 253-room W Seoul, to the 40,000-square-feet restaurant and club for Tao Las Vegas, the sheer theatricality and scale of the design has increased

and was geared toward revitalizing radical design. Realizing that he had an exceptional student, and the limitations of the design curriculum in Tel Aviv, "He said to me, 'Ilan, you have to go to Italy'," relates Waisbrod. He landed in Milan where he worked for several Italian architects and continued more formal training at the Milan Polytechnic University, studying interior design—along with industrial design, architecture and other disciplines—for three year before deciding with his wife, Ronit, to move to New York in 1990 with their newly born daughter, Gaia.

"When I arrived in the early 1990s, there was no work," remembers Waisbrod. He worked a series of interior-design jobs on projects with big clients as Panasonic, Nabisco and Hertz. In the mid-1990s, he was hired for the complete renovation of the massive New York Palace hotel, a 55-story tower developed by Harry Helmsley, as part of the famed Villard Houses. While there, he met Adam Tihany, who was working

on a renovation of the famed Le Cirque restaurant. After the renovation was over, the two would go on to collaborate on projects such as the complete renovation of the King David Hotel in Jerusalem to the Fontainebleau Hilton in Miami. However, it was beginning to become clear that Waisbrod was already beginning to develop a style of his own. Tihany's style of uptown-downtown, tradition-meets-modernism, was not really the appropriate fit for Waisbrod's burgeoning sensibilities.

What would give official birth to Studio GAIA came in 1996. The hotelier and restaurateur Jonathan Morr, fresh from working with Ian Schrager to open the Blue Door restaurant at the Delano in Miami, came looking for someone to design his first big restaurant, Republic. A noodle shop located in one of New York's typically, narrow and long spaces off of Union Square, Republic was meant to be a fast-paced, pan-Asian noodle shop that served nearly 1,000 people a day in its 3,800-square-foot space. One of Waisbrod's first

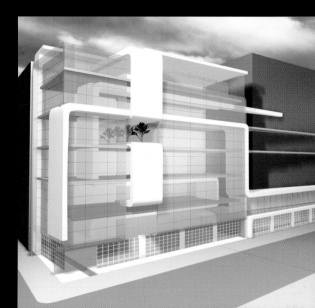

exponentially. Leading up to some of its landmark projects, each space has been an experiment in the evolving aesthetic of Studio GAIA.

In Cafeteria, the space-like surrealness was achieved in the custom-designed, egg-shaped ottomans and leather bound banquettes. In Jimmy's downtown, the modular aesthetic would begin to appear, and take advantage of the firm's use of stark colors in candy-apple red and black, which it would later exploit in the Wave Restaurant in Chicago, and in the rooms of the W Seoul. In BondSt, the modern, east-meets-west aesthetic of the Japanese restaurant would arise again in the design for Tao Las Vegas, which is largely baroque in its handling of Buddhist imagery, exotic elements and nightclub panache.

With every client, Studio GAIA has somehow managed to express a certain appropriateness to match the needs of the client's business. "If you have a strong concept, you can put ideas in more conservative companies also," says Waisbrod. To inject clients with a dose of his own values—and getting them to accept it—has made Waisbrod a true iconoclast in his field.

Even for an adventurous brand like the W hotels, which began with its first operation in New York in 1998, Studio GAIA was able to inject energy into a much-celebrated brand. "To interview at the W, I came with my orange clothes and my long hair, and they thought I was just another punk," he recalls later, in humor. For the W hotels, Waisbrod designed two major properties, in succession—W Mexico, which opened in 2003, and W Seoul, which opened in 2004. While his first project for the W, the Wave restaurant in Chicago, was, in a sense, an audition for the brand, the two complete hotel programs were monstrous endeavors that saw Waisbrod and the Studio GAIA team brings together, and squeeze out many of the best ideas the firm had to offer.

As progressive and hip of a hotel chain as the W, the company had used designers such as Yabu Pushelberg and the Rockwell Group to create their landmark properties, especially those

in New York. In due time, from the late 1990s into the 21st Century, the boutique hotel idea had been copied the world over by half-skilled interior designers whose knowledge of leather banquettes, tasteful chairs and wenge wall paneling no longer made the older W hotels seems as chic, or as hip. Enter W Mexico, whose white-and-yellow cabanas, disjointed, backlit wall reveals, and playful, seductive lounges with custom-designed furniture would chart new territory for the brand.

While the hotels were a veritable carte-blanche project for the design firm, Waisbrod and his team took it further, creating custom seating arrangements, lighting arrangements, down to the treatments of the spa rooms. "The Europeans have always had a much more renaissance approach to design," explains David Mocarski, chair of the environmental design program at Arts Center College of Design, of this approach to design. While Waisbrod is Israeli, and his office a melting pot of cultures, the training at Milan Politecnico instilled a set of multi-disciplinary values on the firm. "In a lot

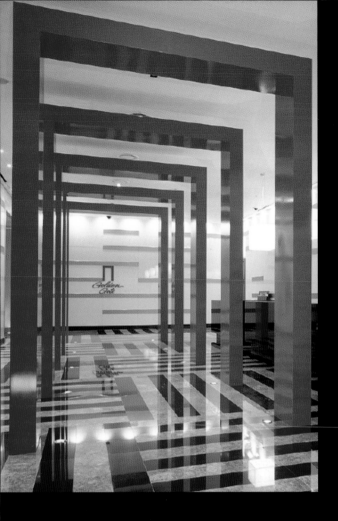

branding, and image."

However, it's not just the large, spectacular, big-budget boutique hotels that receive the studio's treatment. Even with more typical programs, like Dishes, which is a self-serve deli (and which the studio made into a clean and sumptuous space), or the restaurants for Michael Jordan, the results could have come out looking like derivatives of prior treatments. For Michael Jordan, for whom the studio created several restaurants in early 2000s, says Waisbrod, "We managed to formulate those things and come up with a modern design. A lot of things happened there. It's unconventionally abstract," he explains. Elements in the interiors, such as a large, orange domed protrusion, which alludes to a basketball, to screens with projects of the basketball figure's silhouette, the design avoided all connotations of ESPN zone.

Later on, in 2003 to 2005, Studio GAIA also created a large corporate cafeteria for Alliance Capital, the 2,000-employee investment firm. For a company, whose image is no different than other large investment companies in its field, the communal spaces for the cafeteria were adventurous, to say the least. While subscribing to a defined corporate culture, the investment firm asked for something unique to serve the 2,000 employees in their New York office, something that would motivate a collaborative environment amongst its workers. "We were looking for something very different," says Atef Sedhom, the vice president for design and construction at Alliance Capital. "And he was just fitting that category. Ilan was able to adjust to the design style of a very corporate environment. And it was a challenge for him. But he's a good designer. It was a challenge to do something like that, I think."

For the company, the studio created a series of smaller, enclosed seating areas within the 15,000-square-foot space. Tucked away to the side were private dining rooms tucked away for executives. With a palette of lime green, a series of glowing wall partitions, the mixture of wide-open areas coupled with intimate spaces went a long

of cases, GAIA really has that European experience because it's really looking at the emotional temperament of what a space does to someone and creating appropriate responders—such as protruding wall murals and doing whatever's necessary. That's why there's so much success in terms of space in general."

In the case of the iconic W hotel brand, Studio GAIA charted newer territory that did away with the eclecticism of Philippe Starck, or the proto-traditional modern grandeur of David Rockwell. In its place was a brand new design language that derived a bit from the space age, a bit of night-club decadence, a bit of 21st Century glamour, and culled 100 percent from the philosophy of Studio GAIA. "However, [interiors] do not always take advantage of the various disciplines. More unlikely a spectacular interior is not coming straight from architect," says Mocarski. "It's coming from designers with cross-disciplinary and brand experience, and involves understanding graphics,

way in imparting the company's values—transparent and open—to all of its employees. "We never had a dining area for people to see each other," says Atef. "Definitely, it was a very successful project. But you can tell people can see each other. We never had that opportunity for people to have in that big one place. People who never had lunch with each other, they can now do it."

What has defined the work of Studio GAIA is its ability to create, for a client, a vision that exceeds what they have even envisioned for their own brand. The firm has been able to do this with a combination of a talent for visual flair, the commitment to carry out an interior through the details of its interior architecture, and a close attention to each decision. If any part of the visual matrix is slightly off, the entire visual affect may very well be off kilter; but on the contrary, it is always just right. "It's just the typical or logical obvious way or looking at that things,"

says Mocarski. "It's a Bauhaus-ian way of doing things. We did suffer from late '60s and '70s overspecialization in this country. The Europeans have never functioned that way," says Mocarski, who has a rotating program of students interning at Studio GAIA.

Even 10 years into the Studio GAIA venture, Waisbrod shows no sign of slowing down. "We were working on solving a design for a house project," relates Leung. "Ilan was working late, until 1 a.m., and went home to New Jersey. He came right back at 5 a.m. and continued working on this design problem," she says. "When I arrived in the office in the morning, he was already there and it was done!" The ability of the firm, and the firm's founder, to create new details, now forms, seems to be a constant drive of the office. From early days of Republic, to W Seoul, to Tao Las Vegas, the evolution is still happening, though with fruitful results along the way.

"I'm struggling to create a Studio GAIA style," says Waisbrod. "People are already beginning to immediately recognize it," he explains, almost modestly acknowledging that after 10 years of work, the momentum is starting to build. Since starting the firm, Waisbrod's practice has changed and the projects have become complex. While there are not many architecture or industrial designers who find it feasible—economically and timewise—to

generate the equivalent of a whole bespoke furniture line—in their interior projects, Studio GAIA continues to march forward, holding steadfast to the notion that to create a truly successful space is to understand the habits of people. With its brand of interior architectural interventions, from big hotels to small boutiques, the Studio GAIA is just one example that for a certain few practitioners in 21st Century, God is still in the details.

Andrew Yang is a New York–based design journalist.

W Mexico City | Mexico City, Mexico

To design the 237-room hotel for the W brand's first Latin American venture, Studio GAIA was given virtual carte blanche to break the rules and create an inspiring hotel that includes a restaurant, Solea, a bar, the Cocoa Bar, a lobby "living room" area, and all rooms and suites. Located in Mexico City's ritzy Polanco neighborhood, W Mexico City instantly made an impact as one of the largest boutique hotels in the Mexican capital.

The design of W Mexico City was key in the evolution of Studio GAIA as it saw the firm interpret the basic programs of the space that it was given. In this project, the firm would create the transparency between check-in space and bar space, making the hotel functions seem like an extension of the social spaces.

The entrance of the hotel is through a white threshold, with yellow in the interior of the entranceway. The enclosure has become a key design feature of Studio GAIA projects—elements of it can be seen in Tao Las Vegas and the Golden Gate Casino—and it marks for the guests an entryway into the hotel experience. Inside, the design of this enclosure would be echoed in many of the hotel's design features, including in the living room where day-bed-like seating provides for a cozy nook; in Solea, the restaurant, where white, enclosed cabanas with red glass dividers would create the private-public feel of the restaurant.

Yet again, nearly all the furniture in the hotel was custom-designed to meet the needs of the hotel. Made from white leather and yellow fabric, the hanging cabana booths in the lounge areas emote the bright yellow of a sunflower, a prominent plant in Mexican culture. The Cocoa Bar's curvaceous theme is established through C-shaped seating that seems to fit around the circular tables. The desks and seats in the rooms were all custom-designed and manufactured to maximize work space and accommodate guests.

More importantly, Studio GAIA was able to create an interior that was ultimately about a glamorous but modern interpretation of a hotel for both a Latin and international clientele. While eschewing obvious cues to Mexican architecture, the bright colors and almost surreal lighting treatments hint at the reverence to Luis Barragan and a Mexican tradition.

Lobby Designed with pure sensory indulgence in mind, Spa Room offers luxurious contentment. Soul-soothing shades of gray, white, and natural wood juxtaposed with a dramatically placed spa bath next to floor-to-ceiling windows, results in a breathtaking experience. Complementing the journey are various scents, candles and in-room therapies, which promise to make even the most hardened traveler swoon with delight.

Reception Lobby For the main reception area in the hotel, a reception area, clad in black lava stone, includes the bar area which is set right near the check-in desk. It immediately established the buzzy, nightclub atmosphere when guests enter into the hotel. To the right of the space, the open "living room"

Solea Restaurant From the lobby, visitors can spot the 12-seat dining room of the Solea restaurant peeking through; the glass bottom of the private room sinks several feet into the ceiling of the lobby. Proceeding through the lobby lounge, and upstairs through the mezzanine-level Red Room, guests will find a stark restaurant with chocolate brown walls and ebony-stained wood floors, with a white-box enclosure, containing more private dining rooms.

Made of cantera paloma, an indigenous Mexican material, this white vessel creates a cozy space, and is screened in by red glass partitions. Table arrangements surround the white box, creating a provocative arrangement of diners on the outside, and those on the inside.

Nestled in the rear of the room is the Cocoa Bar, a bar and lounge that features acrylic light sculptures and C-shaped seating arrayed across the circular desks. Along with a circular white bed measuring eight feet in diameter, the white leather seats look like cushy marshmallows within the brown room.

Spa For W Mexico City, Studio GAIA also created the spa, which has become a huge attraction for the hotel chain. Clad in floor-to-ceiling green glass, the spa, located on the third floor, is a glistening series of rooms that offers both a calm and soothing environment, while creating an illusion of voyeurism with the semi-transparency of the rooms. A juice bar, unisex treatment rooms, exercise pool and a Mayan style adobe sauna are included, with a playful mural.

Guest Room Inside the W Mexico City, the rooms receive Studio GAIA's trademark dose of color. Painted in a candy-apple red, with sheets that match, the rooms create an interesting contrast with their warm and super-crisp, clean colors. The sleek Studio GAIA–designed furniture is typically generous in proportion. The bathrooms of the W are integrated neatly into the open plan of the rooms, which inspire a spacious loft arrangement. Since most bathrooms have a window exposure, most bathrooms come with a hammock to take advantage of the view.

W Hotel Seoul | Seoul, SouthKorea

For the first Asian outpost of the W boutique-hotel brand, and the hotel chain's second international destination, W Seoul-Walkerhill established the company's truly international appeal, and is unlike any other hotel the W has ever created. Situated in a new building on the Han River, adjacent to the Sheraton Walkerhill, W Seoul, like its counterpart W Mexico City, were the first hotels built from scratch, and not refurbished former hotels like their U.S. counterparts.

Inside, there was ample room for Studio GAIA to create signature spaces like the common areas, the Living Room and the Woo Bar, both of which double as bar and lounge as well as the hotel's common areas. Visitors entering into the hotel proceed to the check-in areas, which are an extension of the neighboring Woo Bar. The lounge directly overlooks the Han River, the mile-wide waterway that separates Seoul into the north and south bank.

Along with the truly grand scale of interior spaces, and lush materials such as the creamy Terrazzo, W Seoul is a synthesis of many Studio GAIA's previous ideas brought into one space; a paradise of Studio GAIA design. The lounge of the hotel features pod-like furniture in various scales, including the egg-shaped ottomans (used in Cafeteria), enclosed cabana-sequel booths (used in W Mexico City), the long, continuous bar (Jimmy's Downtown), stepped-up, bleacher-like seating areas that create a stage-like drama to the bar (employed in the 40/40 club).

With the exception of the Spa areas (designed by RAD, the building's architects) and the restaurant, Namu, designed by New York–based designer Tony Chi, Studio GAIA designed every detail of this hotel including all the common areas, the W Store, a small boutique shop, all 253 rooms, as well the hallways to the rooms, with Zebrawood thresholds with cutaway light-reveals. In creating both a live-and-play environment for W Seoul, the studio utilized the qualities which it knows so well: how to create a posh, night-club–like setting and yet maintain a casual and comfortable environment for visitors.

The 253 guest rooms, nearly all-white environments are mixed with bright touches of red. Several of the rooms are designated as Media Rooms, which feature the signature, circular bed complete with Studio GAIA's scooped-out pod chairs. Attention to every detail is a trademark of this massive project. Since most of the hotel faces the Han River, guests can open and close curtains of the floor-to-ceiling windows with a touch of a remote control.

At night, the scene of the hotel is a multisensory experience of lighting. The scene of the hotel is set by the nighttime view of Seoul across the Han River, as viewed through the generous, all-glass back wall of the bar and common area. And inside, the din of night is created by the pulsating flat screen monitors, flush against the back wall of Woo bar, as well as the candles spread through the various tables within the sea of egg and pod-shaped

LEFT **Lobby Lounge** OPPOSITE **Living Room**

LEFT **Lobby Stairs to lounge** OPPOSITE **Lobby Lounge**

LEFT **W Retail Store**   CENTER **Lobby Living Room**   TOP **Lobby Reception**   BOTTOM **Elevator Lobby**

Woo Bar The Woo Bar, W Seoul's signature bar, is immediately visible from the lobby, and is lined with the check in desk immediately to the left of the bar. At 59 feet, Woo Bar is Korea's longest bar, and has attracted visitors from all over the country. The bar extends from an entry way all the way toward the large windows, which feature full views of the Han River.

LEFT AND OPPOSITE Woo Bar BOTTOM Lobby Floor Plan

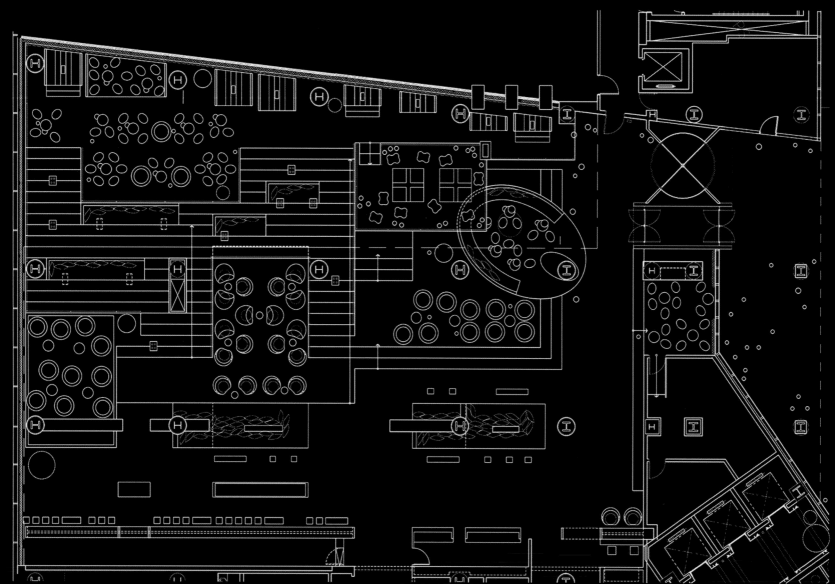

OPPOSITE **Wonderful Room** TOP **Pod Chairs** BOTTOM **Wonderful Room Bathroom**

OPPOSITE **Media room bath** TOP **Media room circular bed** BOTTOM LEFT **Round resin tub** BOTTOM RIGHT **Media room details**

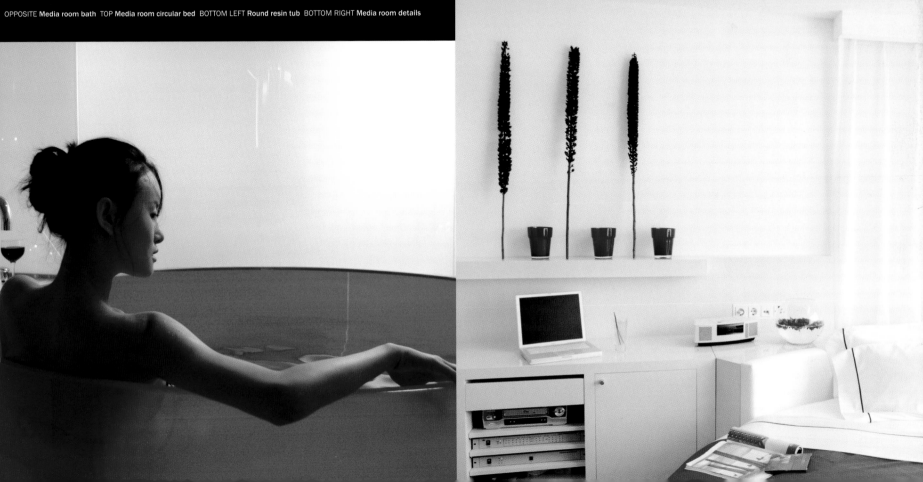

Presidential Suite The Presidential Suite was designed to be the premier suite in the hotel. With long, wide views over Seoul, the suite features a living room, dining room, a play room and bar, wand capture the best elements of the entire hotel. The 3,000-square-feet space also features a bathroom with a 16-jet, glass-enclosed shower. A large slate bathtub is installed in the bedroom.

Spa Suite One of the major attractions of W Seoul is the extensive spa. For the guests who wanted to extend that experience to their rooms, Studio GAIA designed a deluxe suite that is both an extended hotel room but offers extensive in-room spa facilities. A Jacuzzi and circular glass-enclosed shower is an extension of the bedroom. The Spa Suite also features a 12-person, Japanese-style dining room, with the table sunken below floor level.

Republic Restaurant | New York, New York

Since opening in 1996, Republic has become a Union Square institution and one of the most classic eateries in New York City. Operated by Jonathan Morr and Studio GAIA's first major public project, Republic is located on Union Square West in Manhattan, where it draws heavy public traffic as well as a sizeable, young clientele who have it a bustling destination day-in and day-out. In addition to a long, curving bar and the dense seating arrangements, the main innovation in Republic comes with the stationary furniture. Not a single seat in the house can be moved, as all of Republic's bar stools, communal benches and dining tables are bolted to the ground. While not completely new to the restaurant industry, Republic's communal-dining arrangement has withstood its popularity primarily because of the energetic, busy and hip atmosphere—a nice homage to the hustle and bustle of Asian noodle shops, which have heavily influenced its cuisine.

63

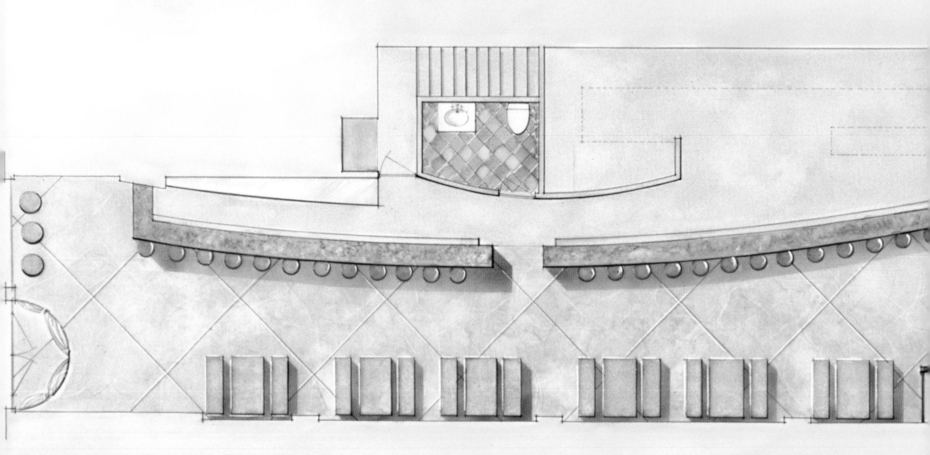

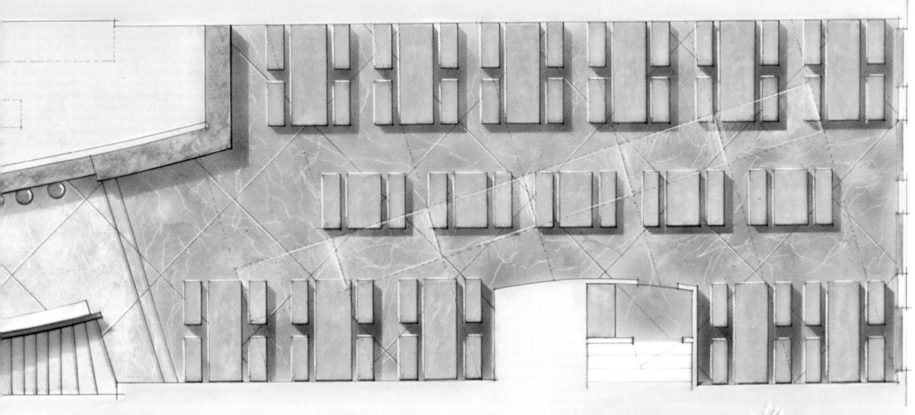

Cafeteria | New York, New York

To create Cafeteria, in Manhattan's Chelsea neighborhood, Studio GAIA stripped away all traces of its former life as a corner coffee shop and gave it one of its signature makeovers. While the tone of the food and service would remain as casual as that of a diner—including 24-hour service—the appearance, anyways, seems to be a futuristic upgrade with simple banquettes and chairs, and two garage doors that can be opened in nice weather. Downstairs, an underground lounge, in a white and dark-brown palette, features padded banquettes and cushy, egg-like ottomans. Because the space would be used day and night, Cafeteria could not only emote a nocturnal ambience, nor could it seem too much like a brunch venue (which it is). A balance was created with the comfortable furnishings, space-age-like forms and luxurious, night club–like atmosphere—coupled with an inviting casualness, a versatile quality that would become a Studio GAIA trademark in future

Jimmy's Downtown Restaurant | New York, New York

An incarnation of evolving Studio GAIA style, the restaurant Jimmy's Downtown showcases the firm's evolving design mantra. Designed in a mixture of candy-apple red and a milky light-beige color, the restaurant takes one color motif and carries it through the space. Custom-designed bar stools, dining chairs and lounge seating by Studio GAIA, create the seamless transition between the ultra-long bar and dining space. Thwarting the ultranarrowness of the 150-long-by-20-feet-wide space, a long, Terazzo bar from entry to dining room leads guests to the large, oval-shaped dining room, arrayed with red banquettes on its perimeter. A forest of candy-apple red columns are scattered through out the space, along with low-lying, reconfigurable modular lounge seating—appropriate for the low-ceilinged bar space.

LEFT TOP **Oval dining room**
BOTTOM AND OPPOSITE **Main bar**

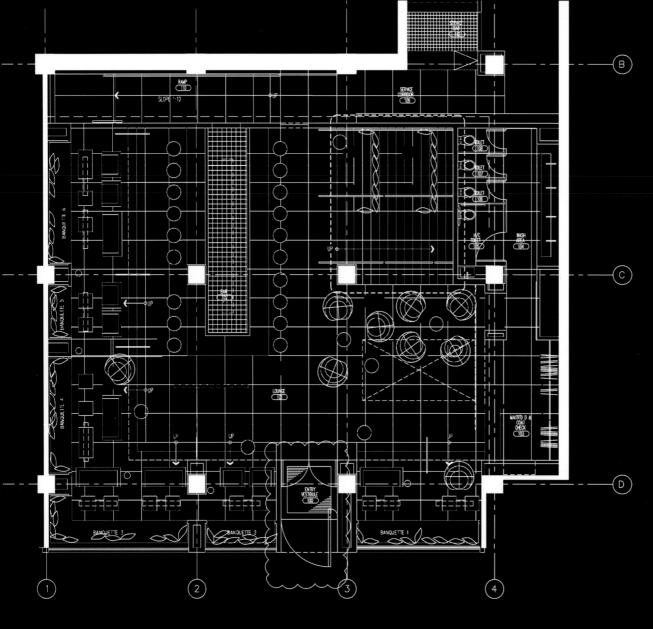

40 40 Jay-Z Club | New York, New York

Opened at a time when big nightclubs were beginning to dominate Manhattan nightlife once again, hip-hop star and music mogul Jay-Z wanted to create his own destination, the 40/40 club. Located in New York's Flatiron district, the 40/40 club is Studio GAIA's version of what a modern sports bar should be. Instead of hip-hop hedonism and the typical bling-bling materials, the studio gave the space a dark and seductive tone that looks more like a Miami nightclub than the ESPN Zone. Floor-to-ceiling poles suspend flat-screen monitors and Studio GAIA egg chairs in the open lounge area, while bleacher-like steps create seating for a larger audience. Private booths tucked away to the alternate side of the bleachers ensure that the sport of spectatorship is not only happening on screen, but within the space as well.

23 Michael Jordan | Chapel Hill, North Carolina

How does one translate the image of such a magnanimous basketball star as Michael Jordan into a modern restaurant concept? Instead of opting for a Planet Hollywood–clone or an NBA version of the Hard Rock Café, Studio GAIA created a space that was an homage to the basketball star without having to use literal motifs. Circular and oval-shaped spaces were carved out of the restaurant, in Chapel Hill, North Carolina. As white chairs paired with elegant black tables are arrayed through the space, a red flourish in the form of a semi-circle on the ceiling frames a large, orange convex dome that—while it doesn't scream basketball—makes the statement in a simple gesture.

TOP **Main dining area** BOTTOM LEFT **Banquette seating** BOTTOM RIGHT **Main dining ceiling feature**
OPPOSITE **Main dining**

BondSt | New York, New York

Defining the essence of a modern Japanese restaurant was the challenge for BondSt, a three-level restaurant in the NoLiTa neighborhood of Manhattan. Designed for the same client as Republic, BondSt mixes more traditional materials and a low-key, earth-tone based color palette to create a simple balance between East-West, and traditional-modern sensibilities. The multi-levels of BondSt include formal dining on the second floor, casual dining on the main, first floor, and a bar and lounge on the bottom, below-grade level. Since BondSt is housed in a New York town house on a cobblestone-lined street of the same name, the existing floors were narrow and the ceiling heights were not generous. To create a dim, cozy environment, with private nooks and intimate seating areas, Studio GAIA opted for a dark stained floor, brown leather banquettes and wall partitions, consisting of think wooden beams, spaced apart, so that the feel is private—but not claustrophobic.

TOP **Sushi bar** BOTTOM LEFT **Dining room details** BOTTOM RIGHT **Private dining room** OPPOSITE **Main dining room**

Wave Restaurant | Chicago, Illinois

After completing several high-profile restaurants such as BondSt and Rep
GAIA got a call from Starwood Hotels, owner of the W chain, to create a rest
latest property, W Chicago Lakeshore. For the Wave, Studio GAIA created a re
bar that was subdued in its light gray and slate color palette, with the one e
wide, red ribbon, which cuts across the top of the ceiling and swerves downwa
of a long, communal dining table. While the firm wanted to install a fireplace
of the restaurant—to offset those cold Chicago winters on the lake—the prosp
a chimney through the building was quite nearly impossible. Instead, a floatin

OPPOSITE **Main bar** TOP **Artist rendering** BOTTOM **Main dining**

The Carriage House | New York, New York

To convert a 2,000-square-foot former carriage house into a new restaurant, Studio GAIA created a bright environment with yellow furniture mixed with rich, stained-oak floors. Inside the Carriage House, the brick wall was left exposed and painted white, while a large environmental graphic of a desert landscape, complete with cacti, covers the other wall. The dining levels are set back—each of the two dining platforms are raised progressively higher from the main floor; and the back reveals a large light well of a skylight. One of the whimsical features of the space is a long, bright yellow oval table—a surfboard, essentially, suspended from the ceiling from several strategically hung cables that acts as another perch for drinks. Surfboards, dessert, cacti and sun? The décor may evoke Palm Springs quicker than you can order a Cosmo.

OPPOSITE **View from Mezzanine dining to restaurant** TOP AND BOTTOM **View from Mezzanine dining to main space**

Michael Jordan's Steak House | Uncasville, Connecticut

Michael Jordan's Steakhouse, a restaurant located in the massive Mohegan Sun Casino in Connecticut, was designed back to back with his 23 restaurants. Mixing leather club chairs and wooden benches, the design successfully integrated the idea of a traditional steakhouse, with dark, brown tones, but mixed with modern elements, like illuminated wall panels. The main challenge of the design was to create an intimate atmosphere in the large space, which was accomplished with vertical, floor-to-ceiling leather partitions situated sporadically around the dining room and the bar. Diners could see parts of the space, and not perceive others, so that the restaurant never felt too empty or too crowded. Like Studio GAIA's other restaurants for Michael Jordan, the idea was to present a serious interpretation of the Michael Jordan brand, and avoid all connotations to a theme

emi Restaurant | Boca Raton, Florida

usion restaurant located in Boca Raton, Florida, the clients of Zemi sought to create a

tinct modern atmosphere for their adventurous cuisine. The main element of Zemi is

openness. The large open space was divided into a dining area and bar with a series

floating wall partitions, which also separates the open kitchen area. With a kind of

dernized 60s inspiration, the materials of Zemi are quite rich. With a translucent acrylic

, and divider panels of upholstered leather, the space is illuminated by rectangular

fers, or recesses, in the ceiling that unifies the space with subtle lighting affects.

TOP LEFT **Restaurant Entry** TOP RIGHT **View to Kitchen**
BOTTOM LEFT **Main Dining** OPPOSITE **Main Bar**

Radius Restaurant | New York, New York

Radius is a fast-food Japanese restaurant that is unified by a central, circular sushi bar. All of the other dining tables disperse from that center, in concentric arrangements. The fast-food concept is established by a conveyor belt in the center, which patrons pick their food. To the left side of the space, a curved bar continues the circular theme of the restaurant. While Radius carried the easy-going nature and spirit of a cafeteria, it was designed in the same attention to color and details as Jimmy's Downtown. To create some privacy with the dining areas, the studio also devised a screening system of slotted wood, with sequenced horizontal gaps that permit some visibility but holds back noise. For the custom-designed furniture, all the lime-green and red bar stools or dining tables sport rounded corners, creating a soft and subtle environment.

Dishes | New York, New York

What fun is it simply regurgitating a trite and unpleasant form? That seemed to be the question Studio GAIA asked when it approached designing a new deli in midtown Manhattan, near Grand Central Station. Granted, Dishes, a new 3,500-square-foot eatery, was going to have more than the normal offerings of a deli-with a juice bar, espresso bar and noodle station-but the basic audience was going to be the hungry, lunchtime office workers nearby. Dishes is what the firm refers to as a "boutique" deli, which offers aesthetic resonances to the boutique hotel but also reflects the specialized and gourmet menu, which changes daily. In the space, a green palette with egg-shell white furnishings—as well as the prints of artichokes running up toward the ceiling—are meant to give the space an appetizing, if not futuristic, atmosphere, and a contrast to the cubicles and fluorescent-lighting environment of most offices. Floating counters of self-service stations are paired with an illuminated ceiling to manage the flow of people through the space.

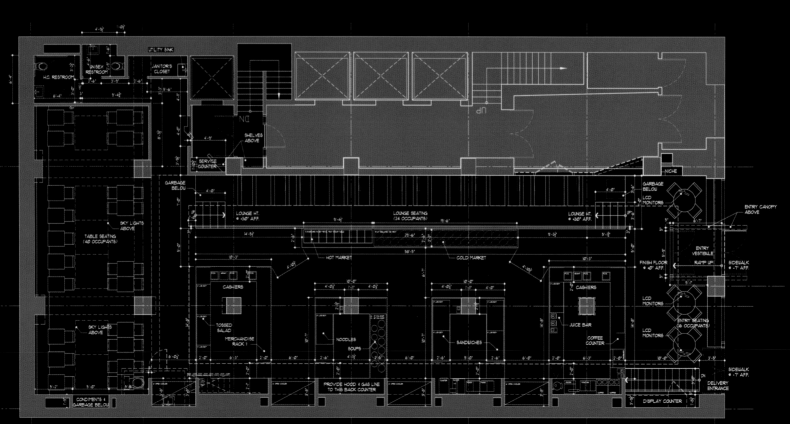

TOP View to dining room BOTTOM Floor plan
OPPOSITE TOP Main view OPPOSITE BOTTOM Salad bar

TOP **Dining room** BOTTOM **View from dining to main space and bubble wall** CENTER **Artichoke wall graphics** RIGHT **View of bubble wall**

Corporate Cafeteria | New York, New York

After interviewing a number for high-profile architects and interiors designers, a major investment company, settled on Studio GAIA to design the company cafeteria of their flagship headquarters in Manhattan. A cafeteria would undoubtedly be a big part of the corporate culture of the massive company, which employs nearly 2,000 people in its Manhattan office. A massive, 15,000 square foot space was carved into oval and circles to create some of the self-service areas—showing Studio GAIA's knack for planning and organizing such a sprawling, social space. Along with open-plan table areas, semi-enclosed zones, where smaller groups-within-groups could congregate and eat, break up the monotony of the office-building footprint. A series of four executive dining rooms were laid out in oval-shaped rooms, each with a boardroom-like setting. An inviting green palette invites the company's 2,000 employees to not only eat in the space, but participate with each other in the communal environment.

TOP **Main dining** BOTTOM LEFT **Glowing green partition and custom round banquette** BOTTOM RIGHT **Beverage wall**

OPPOSITE **Main salad bar**

OPPOSITE Round custom red banquette

TOP Round custom green banquette

RIGHT Banquettes concept sketches

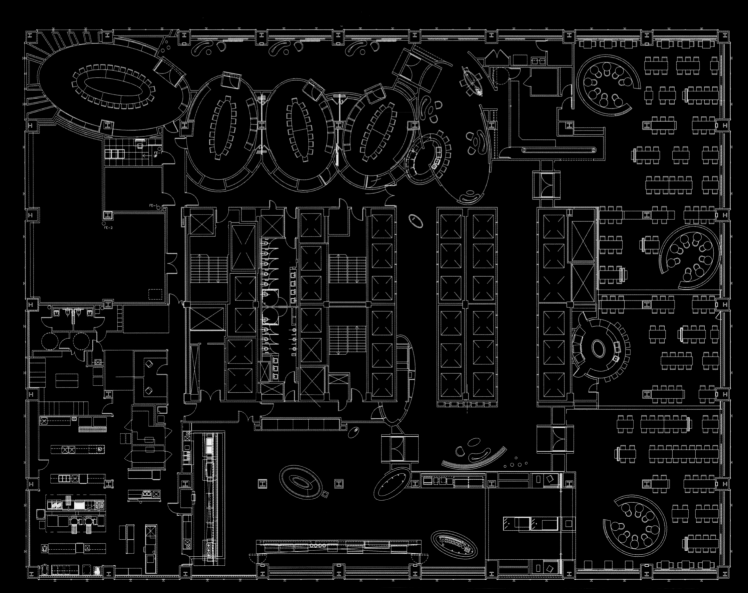

Golden Gate Casino - Paradise Hotel | Incheon, Korea

Shortly after completing the W Seoul, Studio GAIA was inundated with a number of requests from hospitality companies asking it to inject their properties with their sensibilities. The Golden Gate Casino, located inside the Hyatt Regency Incheon, attracts visitors from nearby Incheon International Airport, the super-modern facility that serves Seoul. Under a special provision for the Incheon free economic zone, foreign nationals or other travelers currently in transit may use the casino. A series of red gateways doubles as both the welcoming motif of the casino and the logo for Golden Gate.

OPPOSITE **Casino main areas** BOTTOM **Private room and ceiling details**

TAO | Las Vegas, Nevada

As part of a new wave of trendy hotpots on the Vegas strip, the Venetian hotel has gotten a bit Asian with the addition of Tao, a branch of the popular New York restaurant occupying nearly three floors and 40,000 square feet within the Venetian hotel.

The three-level space is located within the main shops of the Venetian, and replaces a former Warner Brothers–branded family restaurant. Two glowing, red thresholds indicate to visitors that while the interior is adorned with Buddhist statues, this restaurant is a thoroughly modern interpretation of Southeast Asian décor. Upon entering, circular, Chinese-inspired portals invite guests inside into the 400-seat, double-height dining room. With a second level mezzanine which looks down upon the dining space, and a third-level club that looks down onto

Buddha On the third floor of Tao, the Monk bar greets visitors on their way into the club space. It's thus nicknamed because the bar is carved into what looks like the steps of a temple, with each platform lined with miniature model Buddhas, each holding a candle votive. The atmosphere decidedly echoes a sacred space of prayer, that is until

Restaurant Walking inside the new Tao, visitors can either take an elevator straight to the club on the third floor, or be whisked inside, where a 17-foot-high golden Buddha presides over the 400-seat, complete with second-level mezzanine. Tao Las Vegas mirrors the New York space with its scrolls of Chinese calligraphy lining the ceiling and stone tubs of trickling water.

While a part of the dining room is open to the double-height space, the chambers beneath the second-level mezzanine provide an intimate and comfortable setting for the sushi bar and banquette seating. Dragon sculptures, paper lanterns and a glass-case showing off historic smoking pipes give the Asian theme an inspiring Southeast Asia/Chinese twist.

Tao club Inside the club, a large, open dance floor is the main attraction, with VIP rooms, or "skyboxes" tucked to the side. Windows in these rooms over look the main dining space of the restaurant, down through the dining mezzanine and onto the main floor. Next to the elevated DJ booth, dancers, suspended by cables, will perform on a floating platform. There will be no shortage of people-watching, especially given that Tao has already become one of the most talked-about and gossip-page-worthy spots in Las Vegas.

Busan Paradise Hotel | Busan, South Korea

The studio was commissioned to do a complete renovation of the Busan Paradise Hotel, which was last renovated in the 1980s. The spaces include the redesign of the Japanese restaurant, Chinese restaurant and all the public spaces, including public bathrooms, elevators, a lobby, and lounge. The Japanese restaurant was designed to be the like interior or a traditional Japanese giftbox, with the ceilings and walls clad in a red-patterned kimono fabric. In the Chinese restaurant, the firm eschewed the traditional rows of tables in favor of a series of progressively larger oval-shaped spaces that would house private dining rooms as well as open dining areas. Each pod is inspired by a different Chinese word: gold, wood, water, fire and earth—which collectively create harmony within the larger space. Globes of light were hung in a rhythmic way that echoed a movements of a Chinese dragon dance, and leads diners through the space.

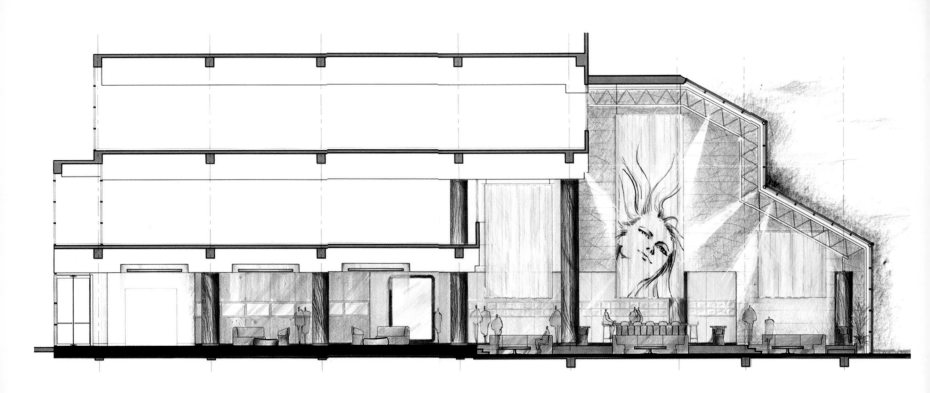

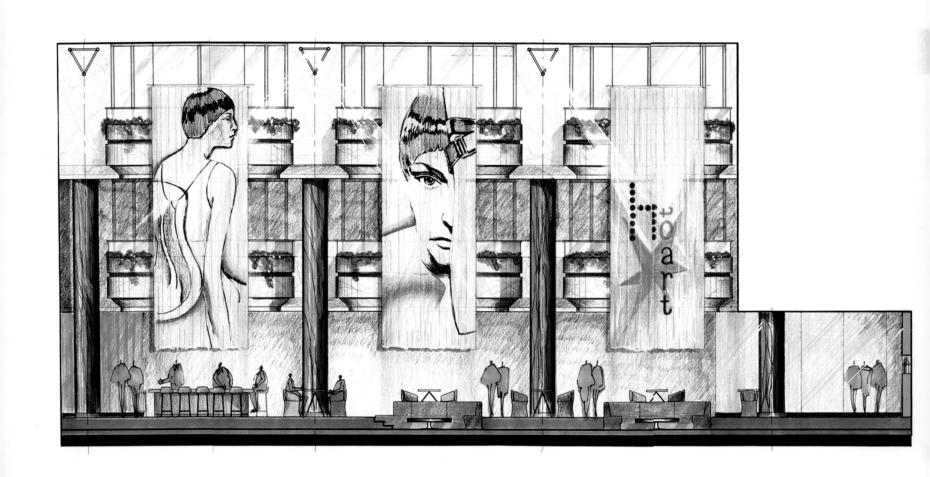

OPPOSITE **Rendered selection elevations of lobby** TOP **Lobby lounge** BOTTOM LEFT **Lobby reception**
BOTTOM RIGHT **Elevator lobby**

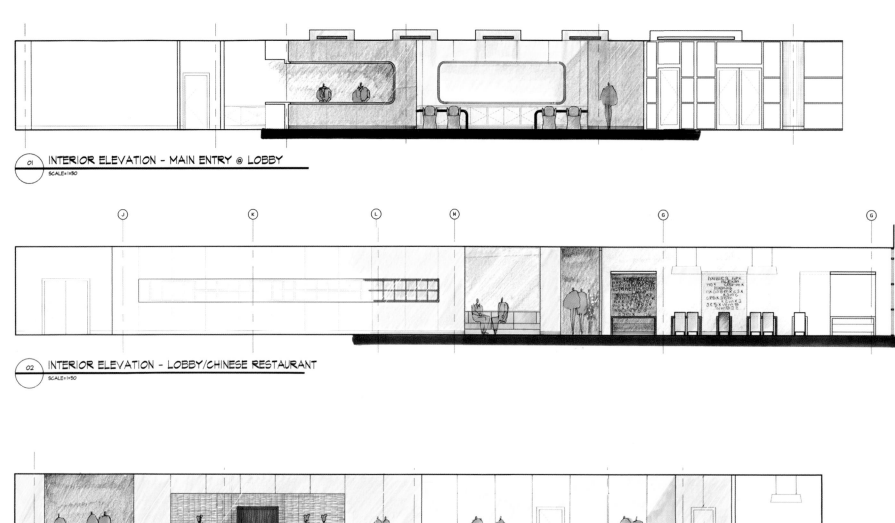

01 INTERIOR ELEVATION - MAIN ENTRY @ LOBBY
SCALE=1:50

02 INTERIOR ELEVATION - LOBBY/CHINESE RESTAURANT
SCALE=1:50

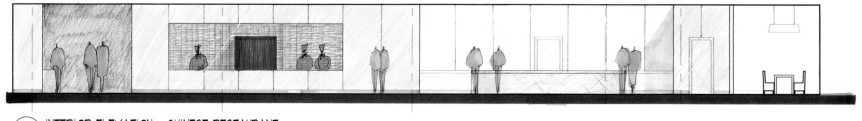

03 INTERIOR ELEVATION - CHINESE RESTAURANT
SCALE=1:50

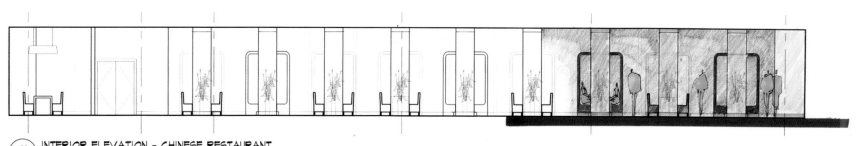

04 INTERIOR ELEVATION - CHINESE RESTAURANT
SCALE=1:50

OPPOSITE **Rendered elevations of buffet restaurant** TOP **Main restaurant view** BOTTOM LEFT **View of buffet**
BOTTOM RIGHT **Custom banquette and dining**

OPPOSITE LEFT **Japanese restaurant main entry**
OPPOSITE RIGHT **restaurant reception desk**
OPPOSITE BOTTOM **restaurant main view**
TOP **View of sushi bar** BOTTOM **Private booths**

LEFT TOP **Chinese Restaurant Reception**
BOTTOM LEFT **View to Private Dining Pod**
BOTTOM RIGHT **Restaurant corridor**
OPPOSITE LEFT TOP **Entry to Private Dining**
OPPOSITE RIGHT TOP **View to Private Dining**
OPPOSITE BOTTOM **View of Main Dining Room**

Costa Rica Resort | Papagalo, Costa Rica

In this conceptual design for a resort in Costa Rica, a series of private villas are nestled into the foot of low-lying mountains, which overlook a lagoon. Each villa is essentially a two-story house, with a little pool for each unit. A number of villas are situated directly in the midst of a large reflecting pool. The common areas of the hotel, which includes reception, is located in the center of the compound, overlooking all of the villas, the pools and the water. Positioned near a rock ledge, an infinity pool juts out at the edge and gives the feeling that the water is flowing into the ocean. The simple and rectangular villas are meant to be spacious and unremarkable, so the forest and the hills create the most dramatic effect. In addition to a private pool, each villa has a view of the ocean.

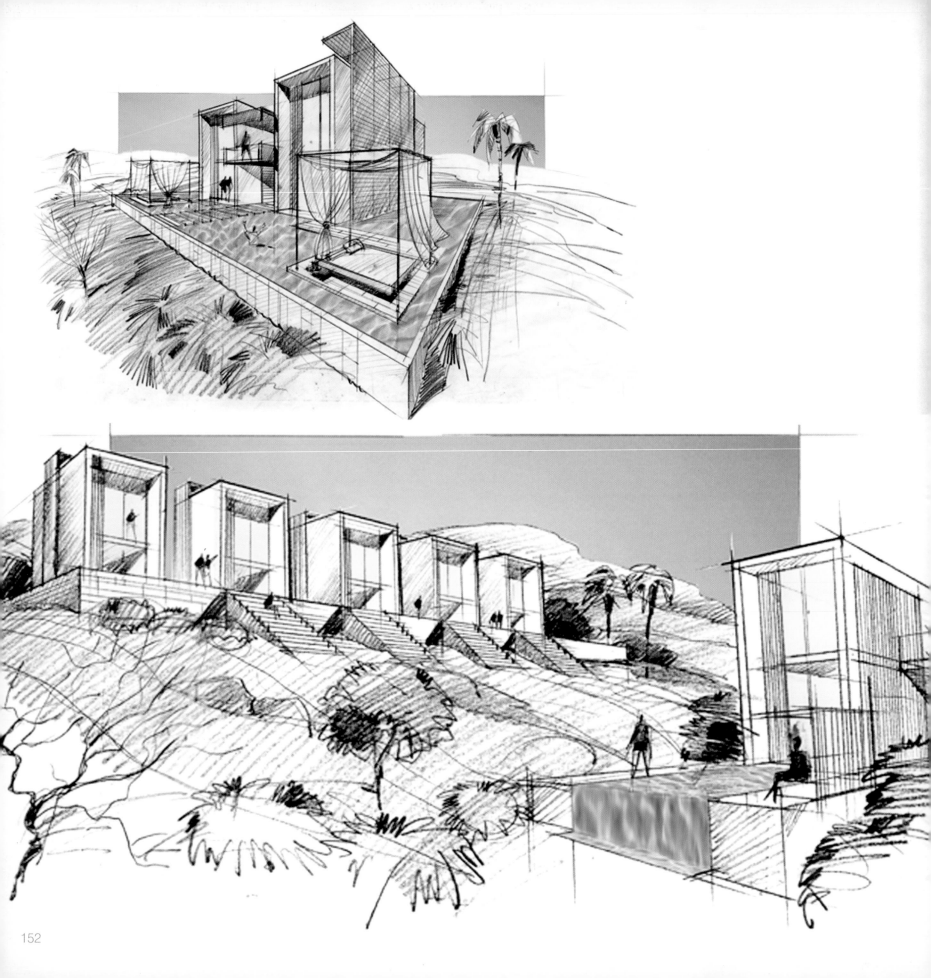

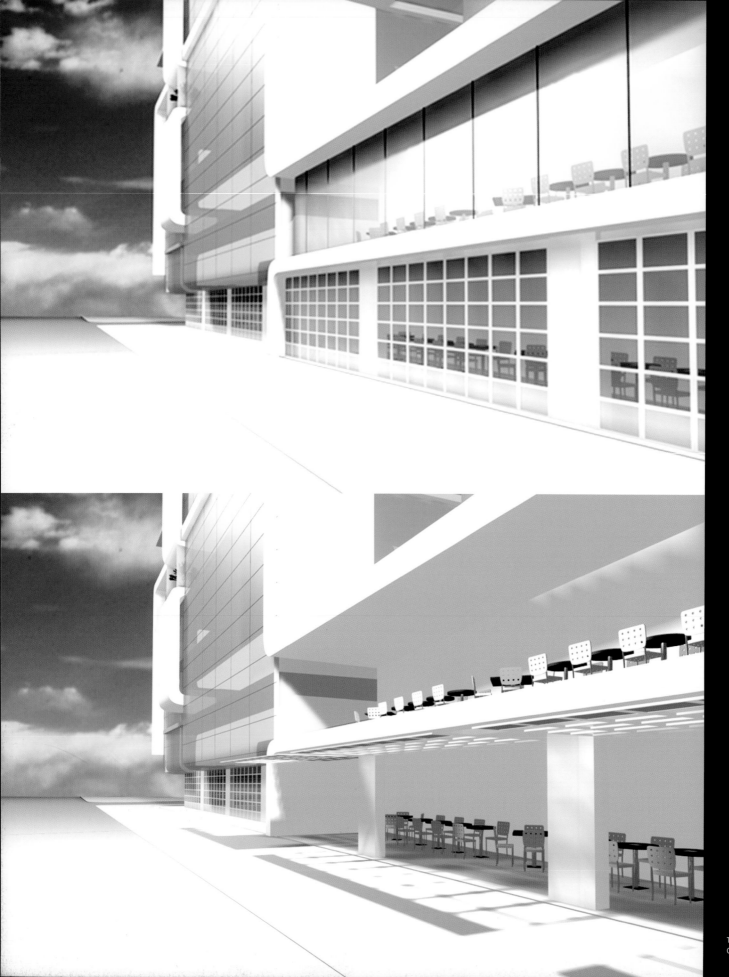

TOP AND BOTTOM Building Facade
OPPOSITE TOP Building Overall view

Cafeteria Building | New York, New York

For the client of Cafeteria, Studio GAIA produced a proposed design for a building lot on Lafayette Street in Manhattan. Designed in the spirit of the Cafeteria restaurant, which featured a minimal design with milky cream and brown palettes, the building was to house another Cafeteria on the street level floor with a lounge on the second floor, and the Cafeteria headquarters on the top floor. Incorporating the indoor-outdoor concept of the restaurant (which has transparent garage doors that can be open and closed), the building's glass creates a translucence, while a flowing strip flows from the inside, clads the building on the outside, and wraps inward again. Since the rest of the buildings on Lafayette Street are old and clad in brick, the proposal for Cafeteria attempts to create an icon and project a youthful feel to the Soho streetscape.

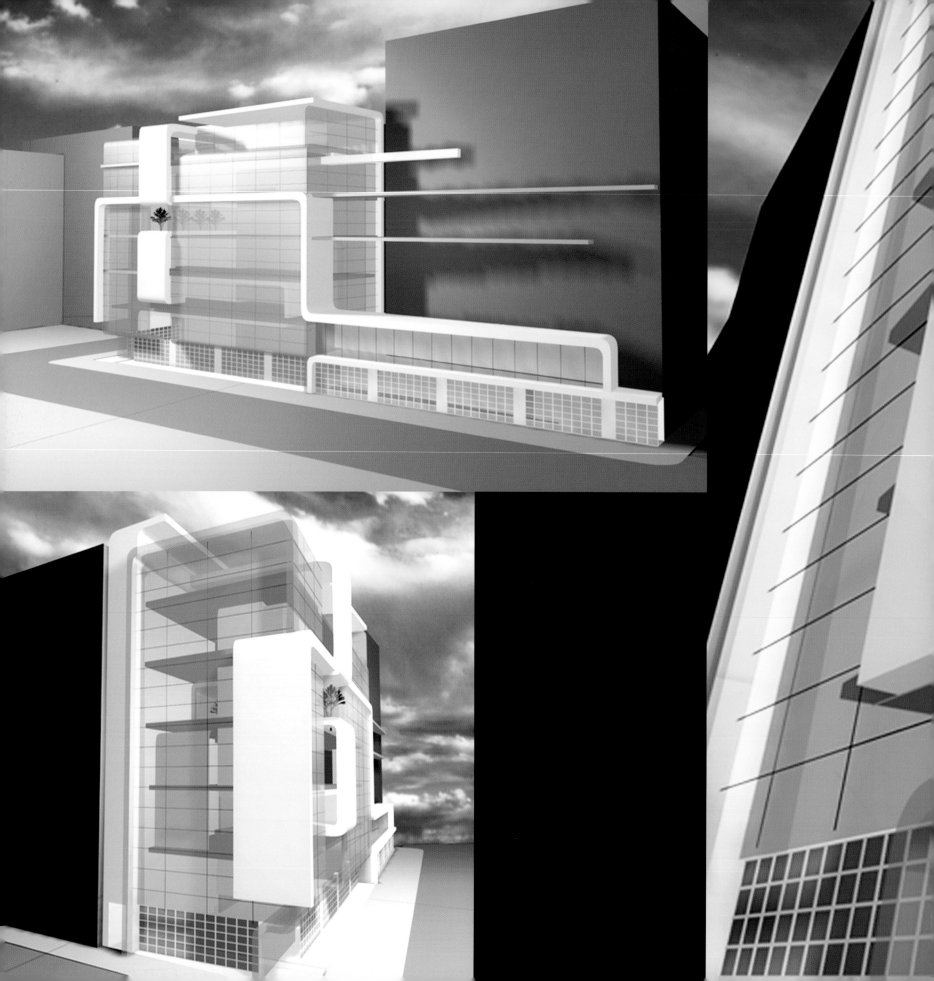

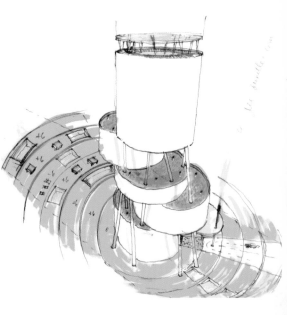

LEVEL 1-7

LEVEL 8-12

LEVEL 13-15

LEVEL 16-21

LEVEL 22-38

LEVEL 39

LEVEL 40-45

LEVEL 46

LEVEL 48

Home Condo Hotel | Las Vegas, Nevada

The Home Condo Hotel is a concept for a new building on the Las Vegas Strip. As a conceptual study, Studio GAIA decided to create an icon on the already glamour-saturated corridors in Vegas. Essentially a tall, cylindrical building, the tower is sliced open and shifted around in various location to reveal openings. From top to bottom, the separated volumes would contain the different programs of the hotel and condo. In the openings where the building splits apart, amenities such as a small golf course, out-door swimming pool and night club would be situated on these upper floors, topped by a majestic, open-air amphitheater on the top floor. Most floors will have some portion of a 360-degree view of Las Vegas. While the Home Condo Hotel concept follows the full-service mentality of a Las Vegas hotel, it offers the opportunity of an architectural icon that is both unique and more understated than the typical hospitality conglomerations spread throughout the city.

Viceroy Hotel | Las Vegas, Nevada

The Viceroy Hotel in Las Vegas commissioned the studio to come up with a concept for a new, modern hotel complex. The studio proposed three main buildings, with ground-floor public spaces and a central courtyard. The main building volumes stand as geometric boxes, with windows standing as lit voids. Bringing in a bit of a natural element to the Las Vegas Strip, the buildings' facades were to be printed with large-scale graphic representations of tree branches, given the main public space a feel of treehouses in a green forest.

The three buildings would be connected on the bottom with a swimming pool in the center, with other square reflecting pools and luxurious chaise lounges spread throughout the space. The plaza within the Viceroy consists of multiple elevations, so that there is a theatricality in the common areas of those who are seen and those who are being seen. Both the reflecting pools and those for bathing give the hotel a sense of a modern Japanese garden, with multiple walking paths.

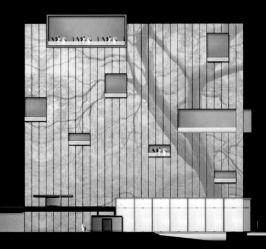

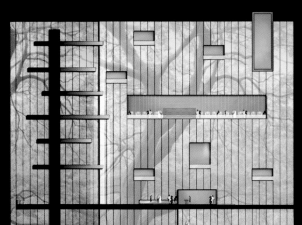

W Hotel Miami Residential Lobby | Miami, Florida

In downtown Miami, the W hotels were looking to expand their successful hotel chain as a counterpoint to the decadent and night-life driven style of South Beach. The development, which encompasses a hotel as well as a residential building, is currently being marketed toward permanent residents, a contrast to the luxury residences of South Beach, which are marketed more as vacation homes. For the lobby of the building, the inspiration for the design was to bring the waterfront view to the interior of the space.

The treatments of the interior mirror that of a yacht in finely grained wood, and striped carpeting. The long curved window echoes the curvature of a ship's hull. A long sculptural wall, filled with irregularly shaped openings, starts from the exterior of the space and penetrates within the lobby to draw visitors in. This sculptural element also doubles as a light screen during the day, and breaks the more rigid dimensions of the lobby footprint. At the end of a space, a shell-shaped staircase leads residents to the hotel's four-star restaurant.

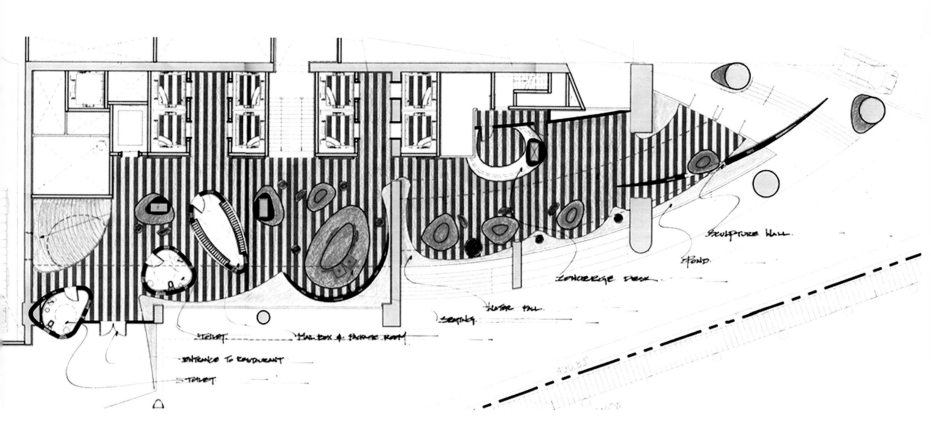

SCULPTURE HALL.

POND.

CONCIERGE DESK.

WATER FALL.

SEATING.

TOILET.

MAILBOX & PACKAGE ROOM.

ENTRANCE TO RESTAURANT.

TOILET.

w Night Club |Destin Florida

brand new hotel in Destin, Florida—located on the coast on the Florida
e View nightclub is a two-story, indoor-and-outdoor nightclub situated on the
chfront hotel. The TK hotel, ready to make its mark as a major destination, is
stinct aura around itself in a town that does not have the benefit of a South
fe scene. All the more important, its signature rooftop nightclub had to be able
itors from not just the local area, but from beyond Destin as well. To create a
the village-like Florida surroundings, Studio GAIA created a 15,000-square-
that was shaped organically, and lit as if it were a lounge located in space. In
P booths, drink rails attached to floor-to-ceiling poles were installed at random
ortion of each pole is lit in different locations. At one point of the under-lighted,
floor, glass doors open to reveal the outdoor terrace space. From the outoors,
the upper, outdoor level of the nightclub. Private booths with one-way glass
clusive privacy, while a window within allows direct views of the ocean.

Aroma Espresso Bar | New York, New York

The Aroma Espresso Bar, a well-established chain in Israel, plans to open its first stateside branch in New York in 2006. The company looked to Studio GAIA to create the first prototype—to be located on a 3,000-square-foot space on busy Houston Street—as the first step of what could be hundreds of other locations. As a contrast to the green-and-brown, Pacific Northwest feel of Starbucks, Studio GAIA injected the space with a heavy dose of color. Stripes of red start from the ceiling and snake down the walls. Long rows of communal tables, as well as long, continuous bar along the window, parallel to Houston Street, comprise the main motif of the café. Custom-designed lamp shades, with familiar, black-and-white photographs that create the soft lighting effect inside. Instead of echoing traditional coffee shops—which usually build around the color motifs associated with the grown coffee beans—the whites, blacks and reds of Aroma create a jolt of excitement without reverting to clichéd motifs.

Photography Credits

Acknowledgements

We wish to thank the following people:

Daniel Barrenechea

Louie Blanc

Ric Bos

Luis Bosome

Pierre Court

Ronald Deschamp

Teresa Fatino

Gloria Fowler

Kanako Fukuda

Emi Fujita

Lev Gordon

Saira Jacob

Clark Johnson

Haryong Kim

Yukiko Koide

Vennie Lau

Elise Lee

Heaohn Lee

Jiseon Lee

Peggy Leung

Kevin Lien

Gabriele Longoni

Moshe Mallul

Paul McGowan

Seungki Min

Jonathan Moor

David Mocarski

Bill Navas

Anurag Nema

Vaishali Patel

Federico Pen'aroca

Pablo Regen

Garret Robbins

Atef Sedhom

Juni Setiowati

Susana Simonpietri

Maggie Talisman

Mark Amadel Thomas

Adam Tihany

Maki Tsuchiya

Patricia Walker

Richard Wolf

Andrew Yang

David Zadikof

Attilio Zanni

Design: Emi Fujita

Staff photos: Guillermo de Zamacona

I began to view the human being as a house that can always be renovated. Like a house, one can repair its roof, replace door and window frames, paint walls and patch ceiling leaks.

However, like a house, it will always be inadequate if it has been poorly designed in the first place.

- Oscar Niemeyer